THE TEN MINUTE MINUTE COGNITIVE WORKOUT:

MANAGE YOUR MOOD AND CHANGE YOUR LIFE IN TEN MINUTES A DAY

PEGGY D. SNYDER, PH.D.

Published by HORIZONS PRESS, San Diego, California

ISBN: 0615873057
ISBN 13: 9780615873053

This book is dedicated to my daughters

--Jennifer and Kirstin--

two beautiful and remarkable women

ACKNOWLEDGEMENTS

I want to thank all of the friends, family, and colleagues that helped me in the writing of this book.

I owe a debt of gratitude to research psychologist and author Larry Rosen, Ph.D. for his helpful and astute editorial comments on my manuscript. I also want to thank author David Hogan for his insightful feedback, comments, and suggestions. A large thank you to writer Hilliard Harper for his helpful suggestions and for finding time in his busy schedule to read through the manuscript. I am very grateful to clinical psychologist Vicki J. Nevins, Ph.D. for her comments, critique, and feedback, and to editor Jennifer Snyder whose eyes were the first to view the manuscript in its earliest and roughest form. Her comments were very helpful and encouraging. Thank you also to my good friend, educator Mary Ann Harper, for giving of her time to read the manuscript, for sharing her thoughts and reactions, and for her support and help in the promotion of the book. I'm grateful to my longtime friend, Constance Lauffer, whose research provided me with creative promotion and marketing strategies. Thank you to educator Jamie Carlson for her excellent suggestions regarding publication and marketing. I especially want to thank educator Kirstin Snyder for her assistance and ideas regarding marketing and promotion. Her steadfast support and encouragement are deeply appreciated.

Thank you to Linda Woll and Lisa Carroll for performing the exacting task of proofreading the manuscript. A heartfelt thank you to my partner, Marvin Many, for his careful perusal of the manuscript and for his patience, support and encouragement.

TABLE OF CONTENTS

CHAPTER IV

CHAPTER V

CHAPTER VI

CHAPTER VII

.

"Our thoughts make us what we are."
~Dale Carnegie

INTRODUCTION

In my 35 years of clinical experience working with psychotherapy clients, I have witnessed people struggle with troubling and painful emotions. Many reported having behaviors that undermined their ability to lead gratifying and successful lives. After months, sometimes years, of psychotherapy, most learned to replace negative emotions with positive ones and to modify their self-defeating behaviors. During the last eight years of my clinical practice, I developed the Cognitive Workout. It's a simple, easy to learn, exercise designed to manage mood and change behavior. I have taught the exercise to many of my clients. I was pleased to discover that those clients who consistently performed the exercise experienced a rapid improvement in their psychological symptoms.

Doing this simple exercise can improve mood, increase self-confidence, and foster a positive outlook on life. These changes in mood, self-concept, and outlook can produce positive changes in behavior. As the title suggests, the exercise requires an investment of only ten minutes a day.

THE TEN MINUTE COGNITIVE WORKOUT

.

CHAPTER I

WHY DO THE COGNITIVE WORKOUT?

You can attain a new sense of well-being by investing only ten minutes a day in one simple exercise. With the Ten Minute Cognitive Workout you can not only improve your mood, you can also feel more calm and in control. You will find yourself embracing each and every day. You'll be feeling more confident, and your confidence will be expressed in your behavior. In time, you will have achieved an ongoing state of joy and peace. And it only takes ten minutes a day.

Happiness Is Great ... But Joy Is Better

Happiness is dependent on external circumstances. Happiness can ebb and flow based on changes in your external situation. Joy is an internal, relatively constant condition. Joy comes from within and feels like a stable part of who you are.

Both happiness and joy are worthy goals. You can attain both. Performing this simple ten minute exercise can evoke a feeling of happiness. Making the Cognitive Workout an ongoing part of your daily routine can eventually result in a state of inner joy.

Emotional states such as despondency, anger, discouragement, frustration, anxiety, or stress can undermine one's ability to enjoy life. For example, a man might want more intimacy with his wife, but his irritable mood is creating distance. A positive change in his emotional state could bring about the desired emotional closeness.

There are times when an ongoing behavior interferes with the attainment of a specific goal. For example, a woman seeks a promotion at work, but her failure to meet deadlines is hurting her chance of advancement. Managing her time better could help her get that promotion.

WHAT IS THE COGNITIVE WORKOUT?

The Cognitive Workout is based on the principles of Cognitive Behavioral Therapy. One of the basic tenets of Cognitive Behavioral Therapy is that what we think directly affects how we feel. Our thoughts govern our emotions. If we change our thoughts, we can change our emotions. As a result, we can also change our behavior.

Changing our thoughts is accomplished via a process called Cognitive Restructuring, a technique used in Cognitive Behavioral Therapy. Cognitive Restructuring involves eliminating thoughts which are negative, irrational, or dysfunctional and replacing them with positive, rational, functional thoughts. Positive thoughts elicit positive emotions. Thoughts which are positive, rational, and functional produce behaviors which are positive, rational, and functional. Cognitive Restructuring allows us to manage our moods and change our behaviors in positive ways.

In short, the Cognitive Workout is a simple, efficient form of Cognitive Restructuring.

But What Is It Exactly?

Step One in the Cognitive Workout is to write approximately a dozen statements that address specific emotional states and real situations in your life. You will learn how to construct these statements using four simple rules. This book contains many examples of Cognitive Workout statements. You can use these examples when writing your Cognitive Workout statements. You will also be creating your own statements.

You will be writing a dozen statements every day. This will take approximately ten minutes. Perhaps, it will take a bit longer when you're first getting the hang of it. Once you become proficient, you'll spend only a few minutes writing a dozen statements.

Step Two in the Cognitive Workout is to read the statements, preferably aloud. It's important to read through the statements at least once. Of course, you can read them as many times as you wish.

Step Three is to internalize the statements. This step takes place automatically. During the process of internalization, the statements become beliefs.

THE THEORY OF COGNITIVE DISSONANCE

Leon Festinger was a social psychologist known for his Theory of Cognitive Dissonance. This theory states that we want our beliefs and our behavior to be in harmony.

We want our behavior to be consistent with our belief system. Similarly, we want our beliefs and our emotions to be in harmonious accord. When there is inconsistency or disharmony, there is motivation to create harmony and consistency by modifying either the belief or the behavior/emotion. The Cognitive Workout brings about a modification of behaviors and emotions. This is because the Cognitive Workout internalizes the Cognitive Workout statements so that they become beliefs. Once they become beliefs, behaviors and emotions need to become consistent with these beliefs. This brings about positive change.

CHAPTER II

GETTING STARTED

What is the best time of the day for you to do the Cognitive Workout? Ideally, mornings are best. That way you can reap the benefits all day long. Can you carve out ten minutes in your busy morning? Can you get up ten minutes earlier each day? If mornings don't work, lunchtime or mid-to-late afternoon works fine. Evenings work as well. Doing the Cognitive Workout at bedtime can help you sleep soundly and embrace the next day upon awakening.

The Cognitive Workout involves writing, reading, and internalizing twelve statements. The next section explains what a Cognitive Workout statement is, and how to write one. It takes approximately ten minutes to write, read, and begin to internalize twelve statements.

Once you learn the basics, you'll be perfecting your skills as you go along. Pretty soon the Cognitive Workout will feel like second nature.

REMEMBER: It only takes ten minutes.

THE TOOLS

All you need is a notebook and a pen. If you already have a small notebook, you don't need to buy one. It ought to be a notebook that you devote only to this exercise. I recommend a small, lined notebook approximately seven inches by eight inches. One in which you can write at least a dozen sentences per page. If you don't have a notebook, you can still get started. There are places in this book to practice writing your Cognitive Workout statements. This workbook format is not a substitute for your own notebook. You'll need a separate notebook to write your statements every day.

THE RULES

Each Cognitive Workout statement is constructed using four simple rules.

RULE #1: Each statement must begin with "I AM". No, you're not going to be describing yourself. You're going to be making statements about your actions and your emotions.

Example:

I am enjoying today.

When you write this statement, you might not be enjoying today at all. That doesn't matter. What matters is that you would like to be enjoying today.

Another example:

I am playing the piano well.

Maybe you don't play the piano at all, but you are about to take your first lesson. You want to learn to play well. Right? Writing "I am playing the piano well" helps make that happen. In other words, the statements don't have to be true when you write them.

RULE #2: Each statement must be in the PRESENT TENSE. Cognitive Workout statements are about what you would like to be doing or how you would like to be feeling. However, you write the statements as if you are already performing these actions or feeling these emotions. You're just not doing them or feeling them yet. In other words, you are writing statements that either are true or you wish were true. As a result of doing the Cognitive Workout, all of the statements are becoming true.

Examples:

I am feeling calm and relaxed.

I am feeling happy and content.

RULE #3: Each Cognitive Workout statement uses the present participle or PROGRESSIVE form of the verb. Present participles end in 'ing' and indicate an ongoing action or condition. They indicate actions that are continuing and feelings that are persisting. For example, instead of writing 'I walk. . .' you would write 'I am walking. . .' This indicates an action that is going on right now and is continuing. Instead of 'I feel. . .' you would write 'I am feeling. . .'

More examples:

I am noticing that I am playing the piano better and better.

I am walking two miles every day.

I am being more and more patient with my kids.

RULE #4: Each statement must be POSITIVE. There can be no negative words in the statement. Instead of: 'I am not losing my temper,' you would write: 'I am learning to control my emotions.' Or: 'I am letting go of anger.' Or: 'I am remaining calm.'

REMEMBER: Cognitive Workout statements do not have to be true. The purpose of the Cognitive Workout is to change your thoughts. What we think governs how we feel. This is a basic tenet of Cognitive Behavioral Therapy. Therefore, it makes sense that initially the Cognitive Workout statement will not be a true statement. However, the way it is written makes it sound as if it is true. And, as you write it, it is becoming true.

So that's it. Four simple rules. POSITIVE statements in the PRESENT TENSE that begin with 'I AM' and which use the PROGRESSIVE 'ing' form of the verb.

CHAPTER III

CREATING COGNITIVE WORKOUT STATEMENTS

Are you wondering what to write? Let's start with some general statements that are useful each and every day.

Then we'll create statements that address specific emotional states like depression, anxiety, and feelings of stress. We'll also create statements that pertain to specific situations such as sleep, relationships, parenting, job, school, health, skills, talents, and leisure activities.

GENERAL STATEMENTS

Here are some useful statements to write each and every day. Select two or three that resonate with you.

You are not limited to these examples. You can write whatever you wish as long as it is a POSITIVE statement in the PRESENT TENSE that begins with 'I AM' and uses the PROGRESSIVE 'ing' form of the verb. At first, while learning the technique, you might want to use the statements suggested in this book.

REMEMBER: Each POSITIVE, PRESENT TENSE, PROGRESSIVE statement is something you would like to be true. But you are writing it as if it already is true. In other words:

I am writing positive statements.
I am wanting them to be true.
I am noticing that they are becoming true.

I recommend writing at least two general statements every day. Here are some examples:

I am embracing each and every day.
I am enjoying today.
I am living in the present moment.
I am looking forward to today.
I am having a productive day.
I am staying focused.
I am handling things well.
I am taking things as they come.
I am coping well with problems.

I am focusing on the positives.
I am moving smoothly through the day.
I am confidently coping with challenges.
I am noticing how well the day is going.
I am feeling fully and deeply alive.

Select two or three statements from the above list and write them here. Or you can create your own.

_____

_____

_____

_____

_____

_____

_____

_____

_____

_____

_____

_____

_____

_____

_____

_____

_____

_____

_____

_____

_____

_____

_____

_____

_____

DEPRESSION

The Cognitive Workout Changes Your Mood ...
in a Positive Direction

There are several signs of depression: despondent mood, a sleep disturbance (sleeping too little or sleeping too much), low energy, decreased motivation, feelings of hopelessness, loss of appetite, overeating, irritability, low self esteem, poor concentration.

You don't have to have all of these to be considered clinically depressed. Having two or three of them over a significant period of time could indicate depression. However, even if you have only one of them, you would probably like to change it. If you have difficulties with concentration, and there is an important task you want or need to complete, you probably would like to improve your ability to focus your attention. Unhappy people tend to have a negative outlook on life. Many of their thoughts are negative. Changing negative thoughts to positive thoughts changes your mood from negative to positive.

Perhaps, you have a good reason to be having negative thoughts. Perhaps, you or a loved one has a life-threatening illness. It is a challenge to feel happy and positive in the face of such a calamity. However, feelings of serenity, acceptance, and inner joy can lessen the negative impact of a dire situation. It is possible to feel 'happy in the moment' even when you are facing the most dreadful of situations. It is a worthy goal to make the best of every day even when the days are numbered. The Cognitive Workout can accomplish that.

Here are some examples of statements to write if your mood is less than positive. Choose five to eight statements that resonate with you and add them to the two or three general statements that you've already selected.

> **REMEMBER:** These statements are probably not going to be true ... yet.

I am focusing on all that is positive.
I am experiencing an inner joy.
I am embracing today and every day.
I am looking forward to today.
I am having a good day.
I am doing something I enjoy.
I am noticing that my energy is increasing.
I am sleeping deeply and soundly every night.
I am being good to me.
I am loving myself more and more.
I am beginning to feel hopeful.
I am laughing more and more every day.
I am having a productive day.

I am feeling good about my accomplishments.
I am complimenting myself today.
I am making someone laugh today.
I am doing one of my favorite things today.

If you are despondent or depressed, select five to eight statements from the above list and write them in the space below. You can also practice creating some of your own.

_____
_____
_____
_____
_____
_____
_____
_____
_____
_____
_____
_____
_____
_____
_____
_____
_____
_____
_____
_____

ANXIETY

Some signs of anxiety are excessive worry, restlessness, feeling 'keyed up' or 'on edge', indecisiveness, difficulties with concentration, irritability, muscle tension, tiring easily, and insomnia.

Anxiety symptoms can be triggered by stressful situations. You can't eliminate stress. It's a part of everyday life. However, you can learn to cope more effectively with stress. Doing so will reduce anxiety.

Anxiety can also occur in the absence of extreme stress. Some people are just 'anxiety-prone'. You can learn to manage and reduce anxious feelings and symptoms of anxiety.

Here are some examples of Cognitive Workout statements to write if you are feeling anxious, worried or stressed. Choose five to eight statements and add them to the general statements you've already selected.

I am noticing that I am feeling more and more relaxed.
I am letting go of stress.
I am living in the present moment.
I am breathing easily and naturally.
I am sleeping deeply and soundly every night.
I am beginning to feel more and more calm.
I am noticing that my mind is feeling more clear and more quiet.

More examples:

I am focusing on whatever I am doing.

I am accepting what is.

I am taking things as they come.

I am letting go of worry.

I am living in the now.

I am enjoying each and every moment.

I am embracing each and every day.

I am learning ways to soothe myself.

I am feeling hopeful.

I am laughing more and more every day.

I am having a productive day.

I am feeling good about my accomplishments.

I am complimenting myself today.

I am making someone laugh today.

I am doing one of my favorite things today.

A WORD ABOUT SELF-SOOTHING

We all have favorite ways to soothe and calm ourselves. We learn them in infancy and childhood. We perfect and develop them in adulthood. The list of possible self-soothing activities is a long one and can include such things as going to a movie, working out, listening to music, yoga, meditation, playing a sport, reading at bedtime, a warm bath before going to bed, taking a vacation.

· Identify your favorite self-soothing activity (you probably have more than one) and do it when you are feeling stressed or anxious. You can also use it as a reward. For example: "I am completing this important work project." "I am taking a vacation." Write these as two separate Cognitive Workout statements. The vacation is going to be your reward for finishing the project. Yes. Write: 'I am taking a vacation' as if you already are. This makes the probability of that vacation happening all the more likely.

If you have anxiety symptoms or are anxiety-prone, select five to eight Cognitive Workout statements from the above list of anxiety-reducing statements and write them here. You can also practice creating some of your own.

_____

_____

_____

_____

_____

_____

_____

_____

_____

_____

_____

_____

_____

_____

_____

_____

_____

_____

_____

_____

_____

_____

_____

TIP: Another useful technique to manage anxiety and stress is the simple Breathing Exercise described in Chapter IV.

SPECIFIC SITUATIONS

SLEEP PROBLEMS

We've already talked about how the Cognitive Workout is based on Cognitive Behavioral Therapy. Research has shown Cognitive Behavioral Therapy (CBT) to be very effective in treating sleep disorders. CBT treatment of sleep disorders has various components. One of those components is Cognitive Restructuring.

REMEMBER: The Ten Minute Cognitive Workout is a simple, efficient form of Cognitive Restructuring.

Here are some examples of Cognitive Workout statements that promote better sleep patterns:

I am sleeping deeply and soundly each and every night.
I am waking up in the morning feeling rested and refreshed.
I am easily drifting off to sleep each night.

I am feeling very relaxed when I am getting into bed.

I am allowing my body to drift off to sleep.

I am reminding myself that I am functioning well throughout the day.

I am letting go of stress and worry.

I am feeling calm and deeply relaxed.

I am engaging in relaxing activities prior to going to bed.

I am noticing that my mind is growing quiet as I am lying in bed.

I am abstaining from napping.*

I am becoming an excellent sleeper.

I am performing a self-soothing activity before going to bed. (See prior chapter for examples.)

---

* Napping is good for us. However, research indicates that if you are having a sleep problem at night, a daytime nap can exacerbate the problem. Your goal is to establish a regular sleep/wake schedule. Try to go to bed at the same time every night and get up at the same time every morning, including weekends. Once this schedule is established and stable, a short (no more than thirty minutes) afternoon nap is fine.

If you have a sleep problem, choose five to eight of the above statements and add them to the general statements that you've already selected.

_____

_____

_____

_____

_____

_____

_____

_____

_____

_____

_____

_____

_____

_____

_____

_____

_____

_____

_____

_____

_____

_____

Difficulty getting to sleep can be a sign of depression. Difficulty staying asleep can be a sign of anxiety.

If your sleep problem seems to be due to anxiety, add some statements from the list of Cognitive Workout statements that target anxiety.

If your sleep problem seems to be due to depression, choose some statements from the list of Cognitive Workout statements that target depression.

The total number of Cognitive Workout statements for any one day is approximately twelve. You can have any combination of Cognitive Workout statements from any of the lists. For example, you might have four general statements, four sleep statements, and four anxiety statements.

REMEMBER: Your list of Cognitive Workout statements can change from day to day. You'll be identifying the ones that are most effective. You'll also be creating your own Cognitive Workout statements.

RELATIONSHIPS

With Your Partner

We are social beings and our relationships with friends and loved ones deeply affect our happiness and sense of well-being. Research indicates that persons who report a close, positive relationship with an intimate partner rate their life as happier and more satisfying than those who report a lack of closeness with a significant other. If you want to improve and deepen your relationship with your partner, the Cognitive Workout can help.

With Your Child

It would be difficult to overstate the importance of a positive parent-child relationship. Within a positive parenting relationship, a child can grow and thrive. In my opinion, raising a child is the most important job on the planet. Doing that job well, not only benefits the child, it also gives the parent a deep sense of satisfaction. But, as we know, there are no perfect parents and no perfect children. Some children present special challenges to parents. This might be due to a specific personality trait such as willfulness or to a special need such as attention deficit disorder. The parent might have a trait or life situation that makes parenting a daunting challenge. The parent might tend to be an impatient person who is quick to express anger or annoyance. The parent might have a chronic illness that disrupts his or her ability to fully engage in the parenting process. Single parents have to juggle the demands of a job, the responsibilities of single-handedly running a household, as well as the most important job of all, parenting. The Cognitive Workout can help.

The following are some general Cognitive Workout statements to improve your relationships. This list of examples doesn't address each and every possible problem or situation. That would be impossible. However, as you learn to write your own Cognitive Workout statements, you can target specific emotions and behaviors.

Examples of statements to improve relationships:

I am noticing that my relationship with (_write name_) is going more and more smoothly.

I am becoming more and more patient.

I am creating a positive relationship with (_write name_).

I am feeling closer to (_write name_).

I am learning positive parenting skills.

I am listening and observing without reacting.

I am being clear, firm, and loving with (_write child's name_).

I am behaving in a warm and loving manner with (_write partner's name_).

I am spending quality time with (_write name_) on a regular basis.

I am verbalizing caring and loving feelings to (_write partner's name_).

I am displaying physical affection to (_write partner's name_).

I am doing something for (_write partner's name_) that I know will please (him/her).

Practice creating Cognitive Workout statements that deal with specific relationship issues or concerns that you are currently experiencing. You can use the above list of statements to guide you.

_____

_____

_____

_____

_____

_____

_____

_____

_____

_____

_____

_____

_____

_____

_____

_____

_____

_____

_____

WORK/JOB

The workplace can contain stressful situations. Perhaps, your supervisor, or a co-worker, or a client is difficult to get along with. Perhaps, your job is very demanding. Perhaps, your work entails many deadlines. Deadlines can be stressful. Perhaps, your company is downsizing and your job does not feel secure.

The following Cognitive Workout statements can help you deal more effectively with work-related stress. If a relationship with a supervisor, a co-worker, or a client is difficult, choose Cognitive Workout statements from the preceding section, i.e. statements that focus on the relationship. In this section, it is likely that you will be writing a combination of WORK/JOB and RELATIONSHIP statements.

Examples of statements pertaining to work:

I am managing my time more effectively.
I am noticing that my relationship with (*write name*) is going more and more smoothly.
I am enjoying my work.
I am having a productive day.
I am noticing that I am looking forward to going to work.
I am living in the now.
I am dealing with one thing at a time.
I am feeling a deep sense of satisfaction in my work.

More examples:

I am taking care of me.

I am developing specific skills and competencies to improve my job performance.

I am creating a positive work environment.

I am creating a positive relationship with (*write name*).

I am asking my supervisor for specific feedback.

I am leaving my work at the office/workplace.

Practice creating Cognitive Workout statements that deal with specific situations at work that are challenging or stressful. Use the above list of statements to guide you. Or you can simply choose statements from the list.

_____

_____

_____

_____

_____

_____

_____

_____

_____

_____

_____

_____

_____

_____

_____

_____

_____

_____

_____

_____

_____

_____

_____

_____

SCHOOL/EDUCATION

Perhaps you are a full-time student. Or, perhaps, you are working and attending school concurrently. Attending college or a training program can present challenges. If you are not satisfied with your progress or your ability to meet deadlines, the Cognitive Workout can help. Here are some examples of statements that deal with school.

I am completing assignments on time.
I am setting aside study time every day.
I am feeling good about my progress.
I am living in the present moment.
I am noticing that my study skills are improving.
I am feeling confident that attending school now is making my future brighter.
I am attending every class.
I am completing all my assignments.
I am participating in every class.
I am getting to know my fellow students.
I am developing a good rapport with the instructor.

Practice creating Cognitive Workout statements that deal with specific challenges you are experiencing at school. Use the above list of statements to guide you. Feel free to choose statements from the list.

_____

_____

_____

_____

_____

_____

_____

_____

_____

_____

_____

_____

_____

_____

_____

_____

_____

_____

_____

_____

_____

_____

_____

HEALTH AND FITNESS

Here are some examples of Cognitive Workout statements that focus on health and well-being:

I am taking good care of me.
I am eating a healthy diet.
I am maintaining an optimum weight.
I am exercising regularly.
I am being an informed and savvy consumer of medical services.
I am reading articles and books devoted to health, nutrition, and well-being.
I am seeing a health care practitioner when appropriate.

Practice creating your own Cognitive Workout statements regarding health and fitness, using the above list of statements to guide you. Or you can choose statements from the list.

_____

_____

_____

_____

_____

_____

_____

_____

_____

_____

_____

_____

_____

_____

_____

_____

_____

_____

_____

_____

_____

_____

SKILLS AND TALENTS

Here are some examples of Cognitive Workout statements that focus on skills and talents that you possess or that you would like to develop:

I am becoming a better dancer.
I am noticing that I'm playing the piano better and better.
I am skiing with more and more skill.
I am seeing my golf score improve.
I am learning to speak a new language.
I am playing bridge with more skill and finesse.

Practice creating your own Cognitive Workout statements, using the above list of statements to guide you.

_____
_____
_____
_____
_____
_____
_____
_____
_____
_____
_____
_____
_____
_____
_____
_____
_____
_____
_____
_____
_____
_____
_____

LEISURE

Examples of Cognitive Workout statements that focus on leisure time:

I am taking time to play and have fun.
I am maintaining balance in my life.
I am taking regular vacations.
I am laughing a lot.
I am laughing with others.
I am being good to me.
I am doing my favorite activities.
I am taking a break from work.
I am letting go of stress.
I am resting and relaxing.

Practice creating your own Cognitive Workout statements, using the above list of statements to guide you.

_____

_____

_____

_____

_____

_____

_____

_____

_____

_____

_____

_____

_____

_____

_____

_____

_____

_____

_____

_____

_____

_____

_____

_____

SOME HYPOTHETICAL SITUATIONS

Let's look at some examples of hypothetical situations that are challenging, stressful, or problematic. This exercise can help develop your Cognitive Workout skills.

Suppose you are noticing that your mood is somewhat down lately. You're under stress at work due to a heavy workload. You and your partner have been bickering. You are not able to find time for your favorite pastime of golf. Life is feeling like all work and no fun.

We are going to write a dozen Cognitive Workout statements to address all of these concerns. Let's start with some general statements.

I am embracing each and every day.

I am living in the present moment.

Now let's look at the work situation.

I am looking forward to going to work.

I am having a productive day.

I am managing my time more effectively.

Okay. It's time to look at relationship issues.

I am being warm and loving with (_partner's name_).

I am planning quality time with (_partner's name_).

I am listening and observing without reacting.

I am creating a positive relationship with (_partner's name_).

Lastly, let's look at leisure time.
    I am maintaining a balance in my life.
    I am finding time to play golf on a regular basis.
    I am taking time to play and have fun.

Now you try it.

_____

_____

_____

_____

_____

_____

_____

_____

_____

_____

_____

_____

_____

_____

_____

_____

_____

_____

_____

_____

_____

_____

> TIP: It's not necessary to group your statements by category (work, relationships, leisure). In fact, it's a good idea to randomize them. Grouping the statements creates a pattern. When the mind detects a pattern, it relaxes its focus. When there is no obvious pattern, the mind looks for one, and thus pays closer attention to each statement.

HYPOTHETICAL SITUATION # 2:

Your six-year-old son is very strong-willed. Everything is a battle. Bedtime is a battle. Getting ready for school is a battle. Getting him to come in the house after playing outside is a battle. You know that your son's firm resolve is a positive trait that can serve him well later in life. However, you are finding yourself growing more and more impatient with him. You are feeling that your relationship is deteriorating.

Let's write a dozen Cognitive Workout statements that deal with the difficult situation of parenting a strong-willed child.

General statements:

I am looking forward to today.
I am focusing on all that is positive.

Issue-specific statements:

I am becoming more and more patient.

I am allowing plenty of time to get ready for school in the morning.

I am incorporating calming activities into bedtime rituals.

I am remaining firm and consistent in my parenting style.

I am setting clear boundaries as a parent.

I am spending fun, carefree time today with (*write child's name*).

I am finding effective new techniques to parent a strong-willed child.*

I am taking time for myself.

---

* There are some excellent parenting books about the strong-willed child. See the list of REFERENCES at the end of this book. It can also help to talk with other parents. If the situation seems unmanageable, you can always consult a child therapist.

Now you try it: Practice creating some Cognitive Workout statements that deal with the above hypothetical situation.

_____

_____

_____

_____

_____

_____

_____

_____

_____

_____

_____

_____

_____

_____

_____

_____

_____

_____

_____

_____

_____

_____

_____

_____

_____

HYPOTHETICAL SITUATION # 3:

Suppose you have a stressful event on your calendar. You have to give a presentation at work, and you're not that comfortable talking before a group. Not only that, it's important that the presentation go well. Your boss will be in attendance.

Let's write some Cognitive Workout statements.

I am letting go of stress.
I am feeling calm and confident.
I am noticing that with each passing day I am feeling more and more confident.
I am looking forward to giving my presentation.
I am feeling well-prepared.
I am enjoying public speaking.
I am feeling confident that the presentation is going well.
I am impressing (*write boss's name*).
I am living in the present moment.
I am enjoying being in the spotlight.

You might read some of these statements and say: "No way is that true!" or "No way am I ever going to enjoy being in the spotlight!"

REMEMBER: Many of your Cognitive Workout statements will not seem true when you first write them. But, as you are writing them, they are becoming true.

Practice creating some Cognitive Workout statements that deal with the above hypothetical situation.

_____

_____

_____

_____

_____

_____

_____

_____

_____

_____

_____

_____

_____

_____

_____

_____

_____

_____

_____

_____

_____

_____

_____

_____

_____

_____

APPLYING WHAT YOU HAVE LEARNED

Now you are ready to write a dozen Cognitive Workout statements that address specific emotions and real situations in your own life. You can use the statements from this book. You can also create your own statements.

> **Remember** the four simple RULES: POSITIVE statements in the PRESENT TENSE that begin with 'I AM' and which use the PROGRESSIVE 'ing' form of the verb.

> **REMEMBER:** The Cognitive Workout statements are becoming true as you write them.
> I am writing these statements every day.
> I am becoming more and more amazed.

If you have used the workbook format of this book to write your Cognitive Workout statements, it's still necessary to have a separate notebook for daily use.

Once you become proficient, you'll be writing a dozen statements in less than ten minutes. This is partly due to the repetition factor. There might be some statements, due to their efficacy and relevance, that you write every day. This is very common. After all, you are probably targeting specific emotions, behaviors, or situations. As a result of repetition, you will be internalizing the statements more quickly. Even without referring to your notebook, you are able to remember the internalized statements. This is great. They are becoming automatic thoughts embedded in your subconscious. Say the statements that you've memorized aloud while you are driving, walking, or showering, etc. Saying the internalized statements out loud makes them even more effective.

I recommend occasionally tweaking an internalized statement that you've memorized. Change a word here or there, or write it in a slightly different way. The mind will notice the changes, and, as a result, pay closer attention to the statement.

Strive to do the Cognitive Workout every day and schedule it for the same time every day. If you miss a day here or there, it's okay. If you find that working it in on a particular day means doing it at a different time, that's fine, too.

Select a time and place that affords you quiet and solitude. Perhaps, first thing in the morning. Perhaps, at bedtime. Or any time in between that works best for you. Consistency is an important factor. Doing the Cognitive Workout consistently is making a positive difference in your mood and in your life.

REMEMBER: Even if you've memorized all twelve statements, it's still important to write them every day.

TIP: One of my clients typed his Cognitive Workout statements on the computer and then shrank them into a very small font. He was able to laminate the statements onto the back of a business card and keep them in his wallet.

CHAPTER IV

ENHANCING THE BENEFITS

In this chapter I describe some ways to enhance the benefits of the Cognitive Workout. They require investing some additional time. Perhaps, ten minutes.

You are writing Cognitive Workout statements every day, and you are noticing positive changes in your emotions, in your attitudes, and in your behavior. You are devoting ten minutes every day to the Cognitive Workout. Perhaps you'd like to maximize the benefits. Or perhaps you have a particularly important issue to resolve in a short period of time. You can enhance the benefits by investing an extra ten minutes. Twenty minutes total. This is optional. The choice is yours.

After you write your Cognitive Workout statements, you read them through. Right? This time, as you are reading them, underline the important words.

For example:
    I am feeling <u>calm</u> and deeply <u>relaxed</u>.
    I am <u>letting go</u> of <u>stress</u>.

Next, put an asterisk next to the statements that seem most important to you. Usually there are at least one or two statements that really speak to the changes you are making.

Now, close your eyes and focus your attention on your breath. Focus on your breath as it moves in. Focus on your breath as it moves out. Simply keep your attention on your breath. Your inbreath. Your outbreath. If your attention wanders (and it will), if you find yourself thinking about other things, simply bring your focus back to your breath. Do this for about five minutes.

Now open your eyes just enough to silently reread the statements. Read all of them, but focus on the ones with the asterisk and focus on the underlined words. In this relaxed state, the statements will penetrate even deeper into your subconscious. This can bring about quicker and more profound change.

Just for practice: Why not try the Cognitive Workout plus this Mini-Meditation? It can be another tool available to you, if and when the need arises.

Cognitive Workout Plus Mini-Meditation

Create twelve Cognitive Workout statements.

Underline the significant words.

Place an asterisk next to the statements that seem most important to you.

Do a five minute meditation using the breath technique described above.

Five minutes into the meditation experience, open your eyes just enough to read the Cognitive Workout statements.

Read them silently. Not out loud.

Focus on the underlined words and the statements with an asterisk.

Close your eyes again. Resume the breath technique for another few minutes.

Open your eyes. You're done!

After twenty-four hours or so, you can evaluate whether or not the extra time investment was worth it.

> **REMEMBER:** You can choose either the ten minute or the twenty minute workout as your normal routine. Or you can choose to invest an extra ten minutes when a situation requires a quick positive resolution.

BREATHING EXERCISE

Another way to enhance the benefits of the Cognitive Workout is a simple, easy to learn, breathing exercise. It takes less than five minutes to perform. You can do this breathing exercise anytime and anywhere. It's especially useful if you notice you are feeling anxious or if you're in, or about to enter, a stressful situation.

It's really easy. Let's try it. The exercise consists of three steps and it involves counting silently to yourself at a moderate pace.

Breathing Exercise
  Inhale through your nose to the count of four.
  Hold your breath to the count of seven.
  Exhale all of your breath through your mouth until your lungs feel completely empty of air.

Count silently to yourself at a moderate pace. During the exhalation, it's most effective if you purse your lips and blow all the air out. (If you're in a social situation, you can exhale normally so as not to attract attention.)

Do the three steps – three consecutive times. No more than three times. You can do the exercise as many times during the day as you want to or need to. However, only do the three steps three times in a row at any one time. Doing it more than three times can cause lightheadedness. In fact, just doing it three consecutive times makes some people a bit lightheaded when they first begin performing it. This is an uncommon side effect, but it can occur. The lightheadedness disappears once you acclimate yourself to the exercise.

This breathing exercise is calming and relaxing. I recommend that persons who are 'anxiety-prone' or under undue stress perform this exercise three times a day on a daily basis.

REMEMBER: Only perform the three steps three times in a row at any one time.

Okay, Try it on your own.

WARNING: Don't perform the Breathing Exercise while driving until you are certain that you are not prone to the side effect of lightheadedness.

LIVING IN THE NOW

The Ten Minute Cognitive Workout can bring about positive changes in your life. If you are doing it consistently, at least four or five times a week, you are noticing positive changes in your mood, in your outlook on life, and in your behavior.

Another way to bring about positive change in mood and behavior is to stay in the present moment. This is not as easy as it sounds. We have a tendency to think about what is going to happen in the future, instead of keeping our focus on what is happening right now. Even if we are thinking about what we expect to occur momentarily, or what might occur five minutes from now, we are not living in the present moment. Thinking about what happened yesterday, or last week, or five years ago is not living in the now. The past is gone and the future never gets here. All we have is NOW, this present moment. Living fully in the NOW allows us to experience life deeply, to let go of apprehension about the future, and to cast aside regret about the past.

TECHNIQUES FOR STAYING IN THE NOW

The Cognitive Workout can help us stay anchored in the present. You can make "I'm living in the present moment" one of your daily Cognitive Workout statements. If you find yourself dwelling on past events, you can make "I'm letting go of the past" one of your Cognitive Workout statements.

There are other techniques for staying in the NOW. If you find yourself thinking about what's going to happen or reflecting on past events, you can bring yourself back into the present with some simple exercises.

Exercises

Focus your attention on all of the tactile stimuli you are experiencing right now. The feel of your clothes against your skin. For example, how your feet feel inside your shoes. How each shoe feels encasing your foot. The feel of your sock surrounding your foot. How the inner sole of the shoe feels against the sole of your foot. Wiggle your toes and notice how they feel in your sock and in your shoe.

If you're sitting down, notice the feel of the seat of your chair against your buttocks. How the back of the chair feels against your back. Notice the sensation of the floor against the bottom of your feet.

If you're walking, notice each sensation as your foot comes in contact with the ground or the floor.

If you're lying down, notice all of the sensations of the bed against the various parts of your body. How the bedclothes feel against your skin.

Any of the above exercises will pull you back into the present and help you stay in the NOW.

REMEMBER:
I am managing my mood.
I am changing my life.

CHAPTER V

MEDITATION

This is a bonus section. Read it only if you're interested in learning more about meditation. You might decide to make meditation a part of your daily routine.

> **REMEMBER:** Investing only ten minutes a day in the Cognitive Workout is sufficient.

There are many meditation techniques. Let's look at two of them: the Breath Technique and the Internal Energy Technique.

MEDITATION: TWO TECHNIQUES

THE BREATH TECHNIQUE

Do you remember the short exercise I described to enhance the benefits of the Cognitive Workout? The Cognitive Workout plus Mini-Meditation? After underlining important words in your Cognitive Workout statements and putting an asterisk beside the ones that really speak to the changes you want to make, I had you focus on your breath. Have you tried it? If so, you performed a mini-meditation.

You can, if you wish, perform a more extended version of meditation using the same technique. Just breathe naturally. Don't try to manage or control your breath in any way.

> Focus on your breath as you inhale.
> Focus on your breath as you exhale.
> Focus your attention on your inbreath.
> Focus your attention on your outbreath.
> Your breath as it comes in.
> Your breath as it goes out.

You might notice that your breathing changes. Perhaps, it slows down. Perhaps, it speeds up. Perhaps, it becomes deeper. Perhaps, it becomes more shallow. Don't try to manage or control it. Just notice it.

Your breath as it comes in.
Your breath as it goes out.

When you notice your attention wandering (and it will) simply bring your attention back to your breath.

Your breath as it comes in.
Your breath as it goes out.

Each time you notice that your attention is wandering, or you are thinking about other things, simply bring your attention back to your breath.

Do this exercise for approximately twenty minutes every day or at least four or five times per week.

THE INTERNAL ENERGY TECHNIQUE

There is energy within all living matter. Energy is constantly circulating within your body. The activities of cells and tissues generate electrical fields that can be detected on the surface of the skin. Skin conductivity is one of the indices measured by the polygraph or lie detector.

Sitting quietly and focusing one's attention on the energy within your body is an easy and effective way to induce a meditative state.

Close your eyes and notice the energy within your body.
You might notice it within your feet and legs.
You might notice it within your hands and arms.
Perhaps you can feel it in your chest or deep within your core.
You might notice the energy in several parts of the body simultaneously.
You might notice the energy moving through the body.
Any of these perceptions is perfectly natural.
All of these perceptions are common.
Simply keep your attention on the energy.
Notice it.
Focus all of your attention on the energy within your body.
Your mind is becoming quiet.
Your thoughts are slowing down.

If you notice that your mind is wandering, simply bring your attention back to the energy within your body.

Notice how it feels.
Notice where it is.
Notice its movement.

As you notice some or all of these things, you are sinking into a pleasant state of meditation.

Do this exercise for approximately twenty minutes every day or at least four or five times per week.

THE COGNITIVE WORKOUT AND MEDITATION

You can incorporate the Cognitive Workout into the meditation experience. Use either of the two meditation techniques described above. Select the one that works best for you. After you are in the meditative state for approximately ten minutes, open your eyes just enough to silently read your Cognitive Workout statements.

Focus on the ones with an asterisk. Focus on each of the underlined words. Then close your eyes again and focus your attention on the energy within your body or on your breath. As you do so, your meditative state will deepen, and the Cognitive Workout statements will be assimilated into your subconscious mind. This process of internalization facilitates positive changes in behavior and emotion.

CHAPTER VI

THE COGNITIVE WORKOUT AND AFFIRMATIONS:

A Comparison

How is the Cognitive Workout different from simply saying affirmations aloud?

Saying affirmations is a valuable tool, and the Cognitive Workout is in many ways similar to this practice. However, there seems to be something more powerful and beneficial about writing the affirmations or Cognitive Workout statements. The act of writing them embeds them deeper in your subconscious and enhances the likelihood that they will be translated into behavioral and emotional change. When we write something every day we come to believe it. It is difficult to feel or behave in a way that contradicts a belief.

Many experts who recommend saying affirmations also recommend writing them down. The Ten Minute Cognitive

Workout recommends writing them down in a very specific format. The progressive form of the verb communicates to the subconscious that the new behavior is already occurring, and that the new emotion is already being experienced. 'I am feeling happy' is a more powerful message than 'I am happy' or 'I am going to find happiness'. 'I am living a nicotine-free life' is a much more powerful message than 'I am going to quit smoking'. Because the first example states that the 'quitting' has already occurred, and the mind comes to believe it.

Some affirmations talk to you, e.g. 'Live Life Fully!' Cognitive Workout statements express what you are already doing. 'I am living life fully'.

Some affirmations predict the future. 'I am going to lose weight'. Cognitive Workout statements describe the present. 'I am losing weight today'.

Some affirmations ascribe traits. 'I'm a competent person'. Cognitive Workout statements describe current behavior. 'I am doing a good job'.

Some affirmations affirm the ability to change emotions. 'I can be happy'. Cognitive Workout statements express stable, ongoing emotions that are currently being experienced. 'I am feeling happy'.

There is a significant difference between 'I am going to find peace and joy. . .' and 'I am experiencing a deep sense of peace and joy'.

Affirmations are effective when they are Positive "I" state-ments in the Present tense using the Progressive form of the verb. Affirmations are even more effective when you write them every day.

CHAPTER VII

SUMMARY

Consistently doing the Cognitive Workout can change your life. By means of Cognitive Restructuring, the Cognitive Workout replaces negative, irrational, dysfunctional thoughts with positive, rational, functional thoughts. Our thoughts govern our emotions. Positive thoughts trigger positive emotions. Rational, functional thinking results in positive emotions and rational, functional behavior.

The Cognitive Workout statement, "I am feeling well-liked by others. . ." brings about feelings of well-being. These positive feelings of well-being motivate you to interact with others in a positive manner. The negative, dysfunctional thoughts, "I am not popular. . ." or "People don't like me. . .", generate negative feelings of low self-worth which can inhibit you from engaging in positive social interaction.

The Cognitive Workout requires only ten minutes a day. Doing the Cognitive Workout consistently every day can change your mood, your behavior, and your outlook on life. Set as your goal to perform the Cognitive Workout on a daily basis. If you are managing to do the Cognitive Workout at least four or five days a week, that's great. You are making a significant difference in your life.

The Ten Minute Cognitive Workout is a maintenance technique. As you notice that you are feeling calmer, happier, and more in control of your life, you might be tempted to discontinue the Cognitive Workout. This would be a mistake.

If you are working out at the gym on a regular basis, you are beginning to notice that you are feeling stronger, more energetic, and more fit. Right? Does this mean you can stop working out regularly? Of course not.

The same is true of the Cognitive Workout. Doing the Cognitive Workout consistently not only maintains the gains you've made, it also strengthens and enhances these gains. Think of the Cognitive Workout as a daily tune-up.

> # REMEMBER: It only takes ten minutes.

REFERENCES

Beck, Judith, <u>Cognitive Therapy: Basics and Beyond</u>. July 2011.

M.D., Burns, David D., <u>The Feeling Good Handbook</u>. May, 1999.

Festinger, Leon, <u>A Theory of Cognitive Dissonance</u>, June 1957.

Forehand, Rex and Nicholas Long, <u>Parenting the Strong-Willed Child: The Clinically Proven Five Week Program for Parents of Two- to Six-Year-Olds</u>. June, 2010.

Greenberger, Dennis and Christine Padesky, <u>Mind over Mood</u>, March, 1995.

Tobias, Cynthia, <u>You Can't Make Me (But I Can Be Persuaded): Strategies for Bringing Out the Best in Your Strong-Willed Child</u>. September, 2012.

Made in the USA
San Bernardino, CA
14 March 2014